It's Melting!

W9-AZZ-241

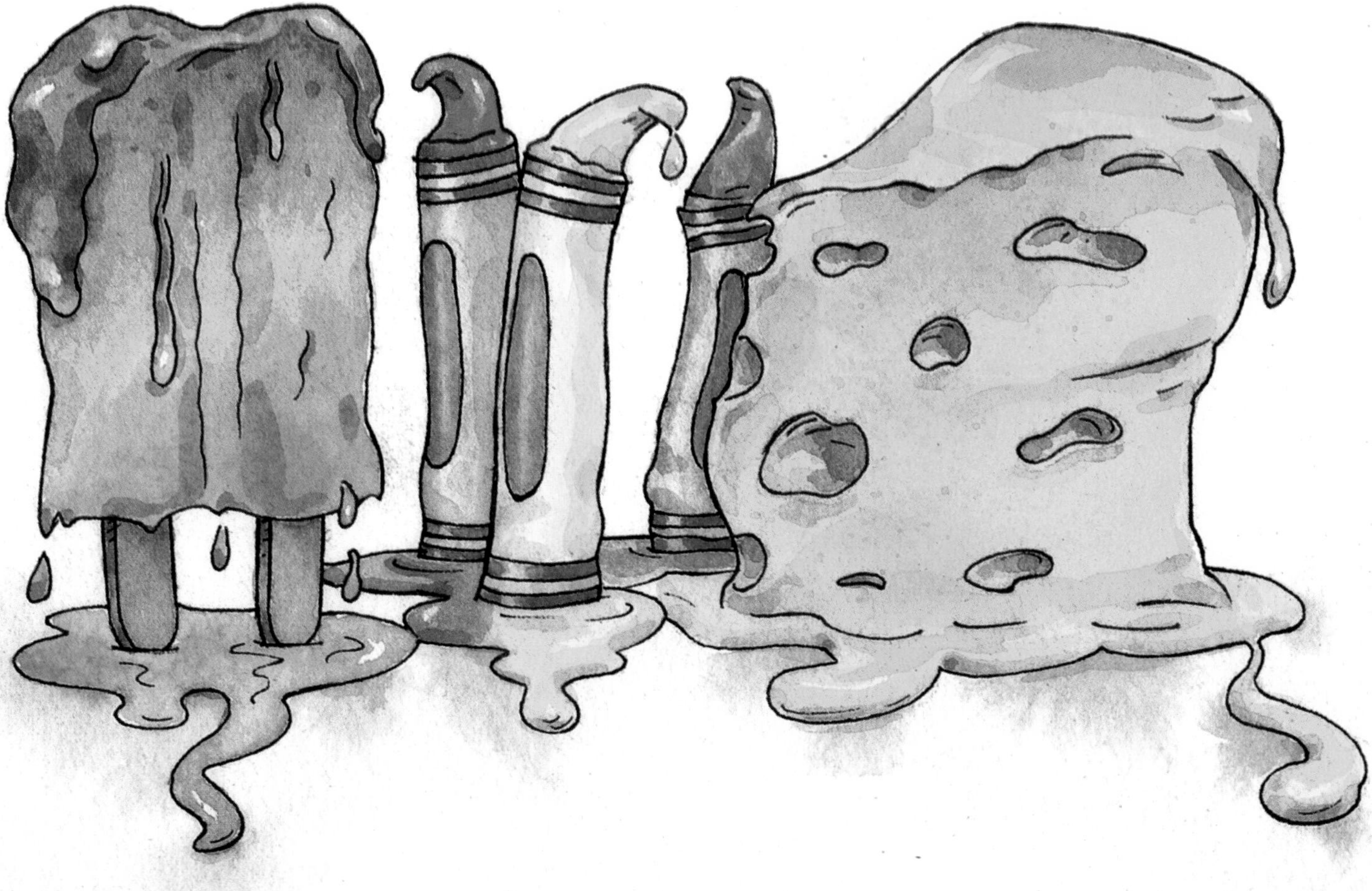

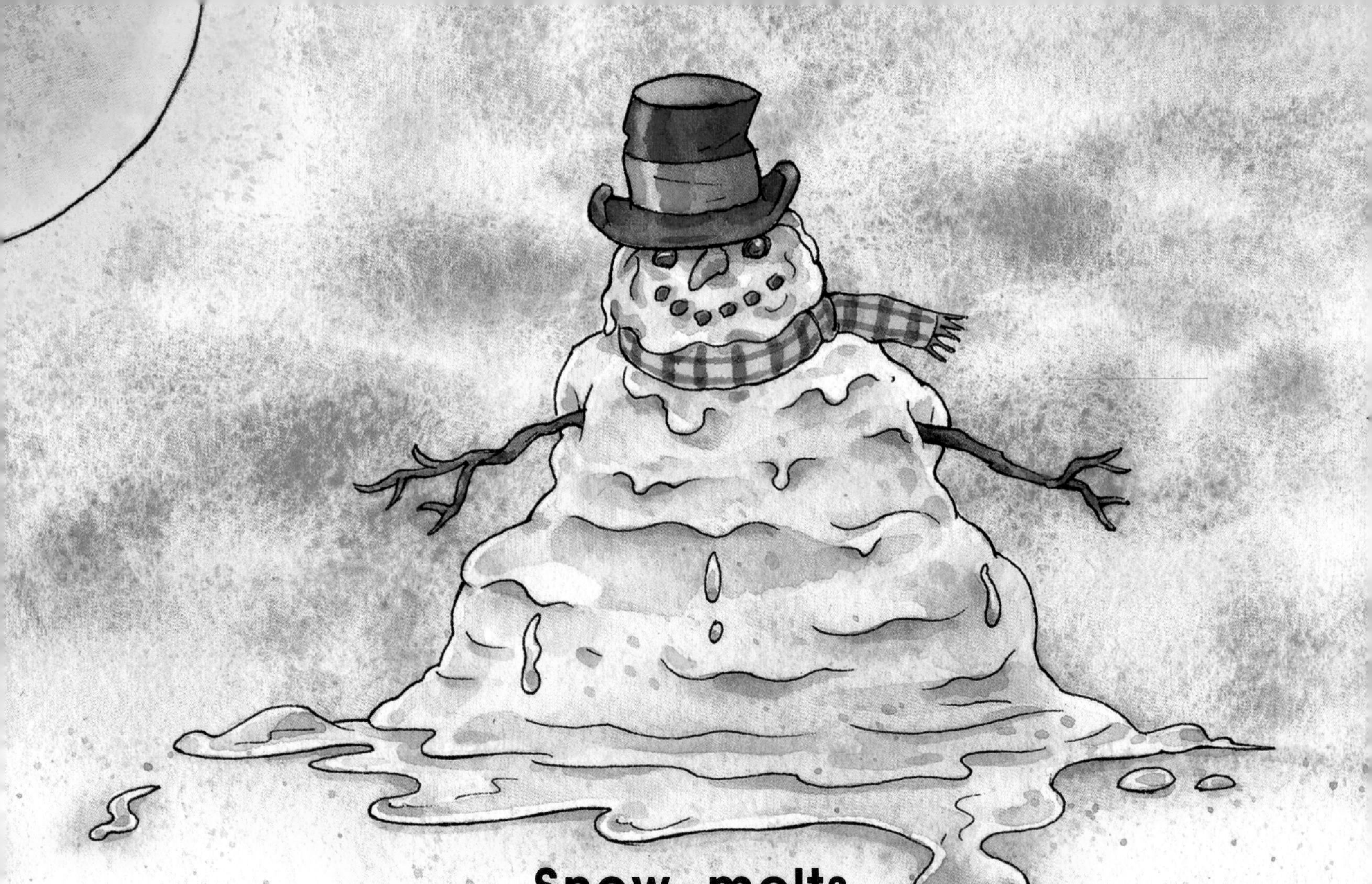

Snow melts.

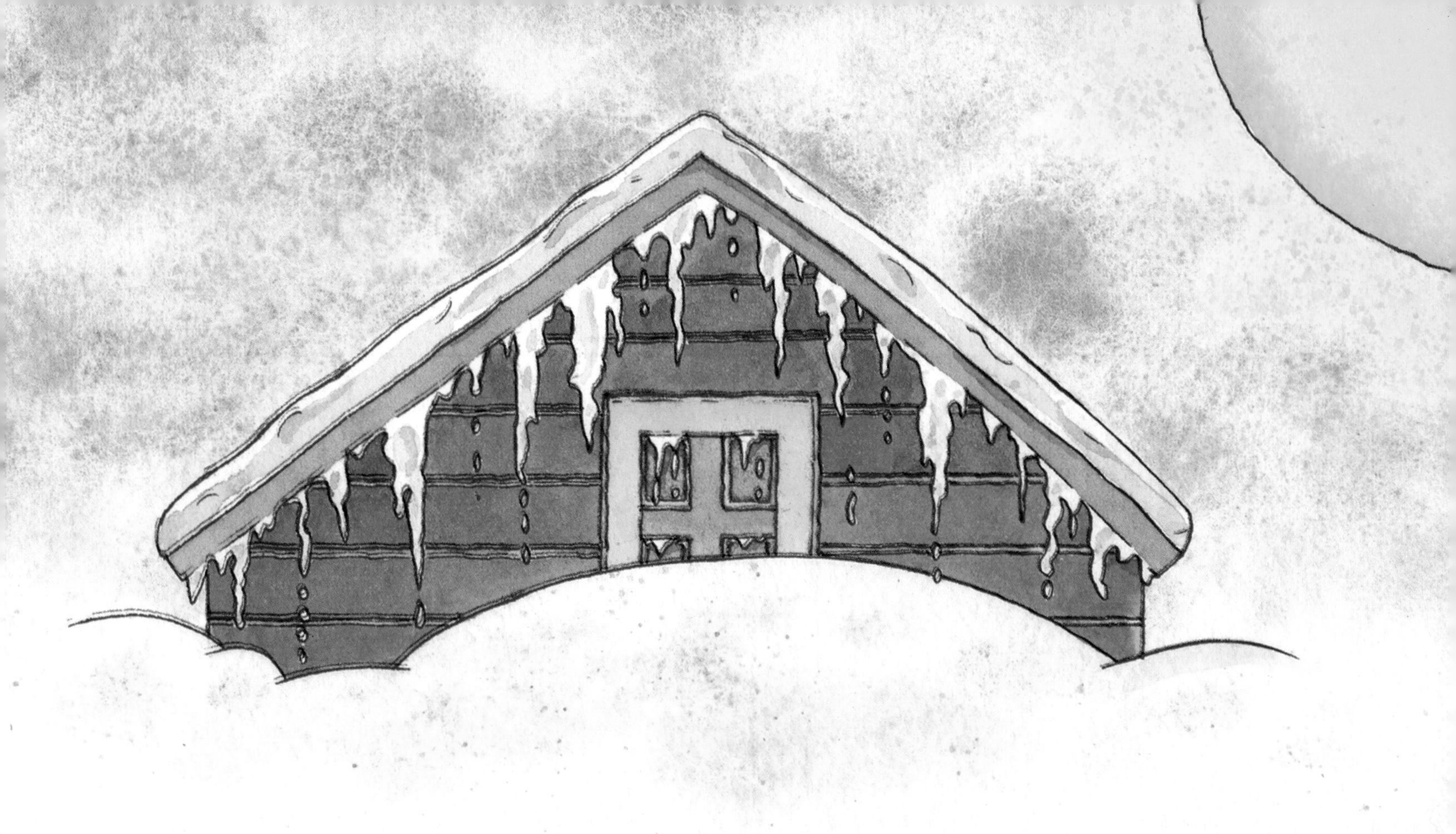

Ice melts.

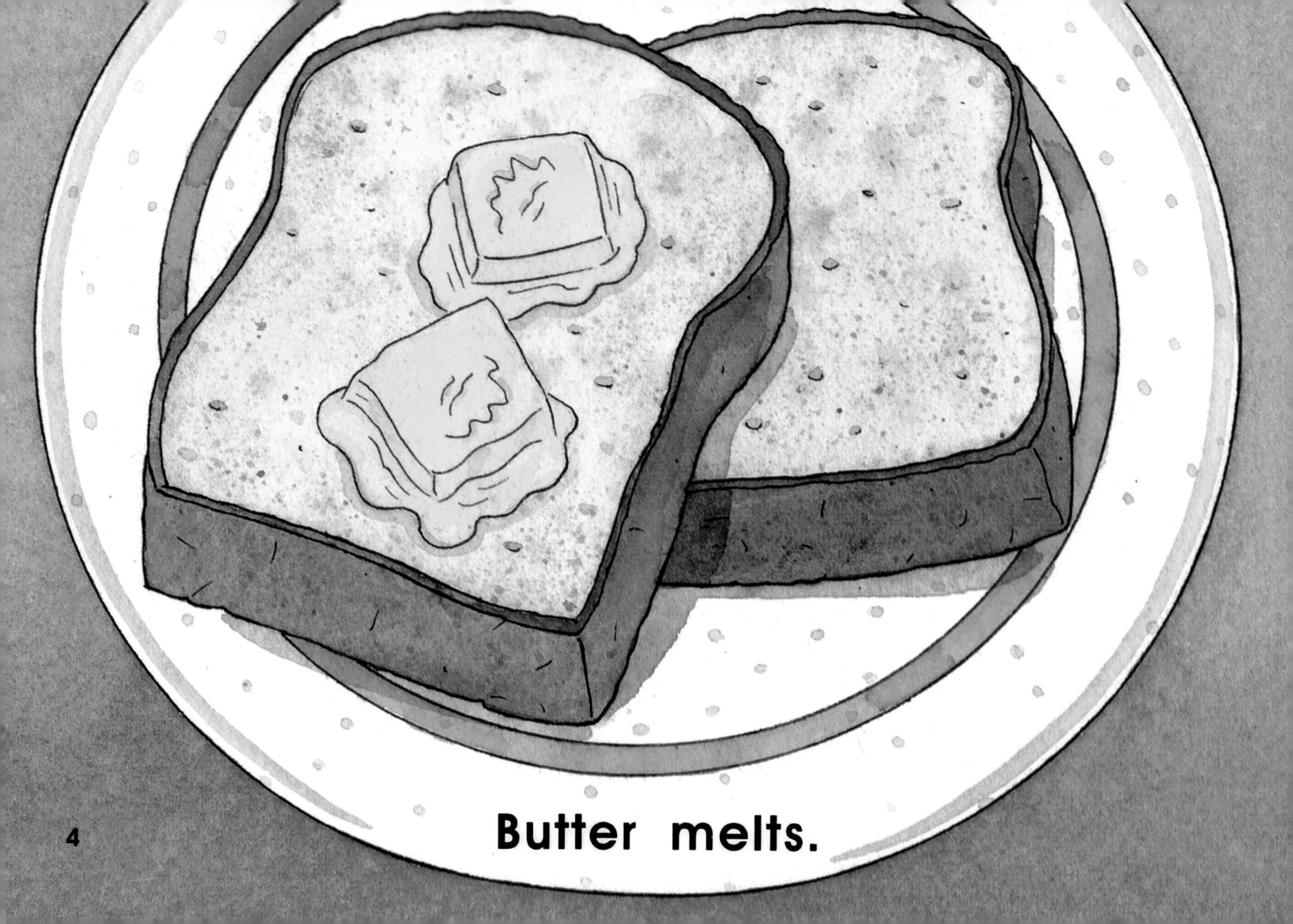

Butter melts.

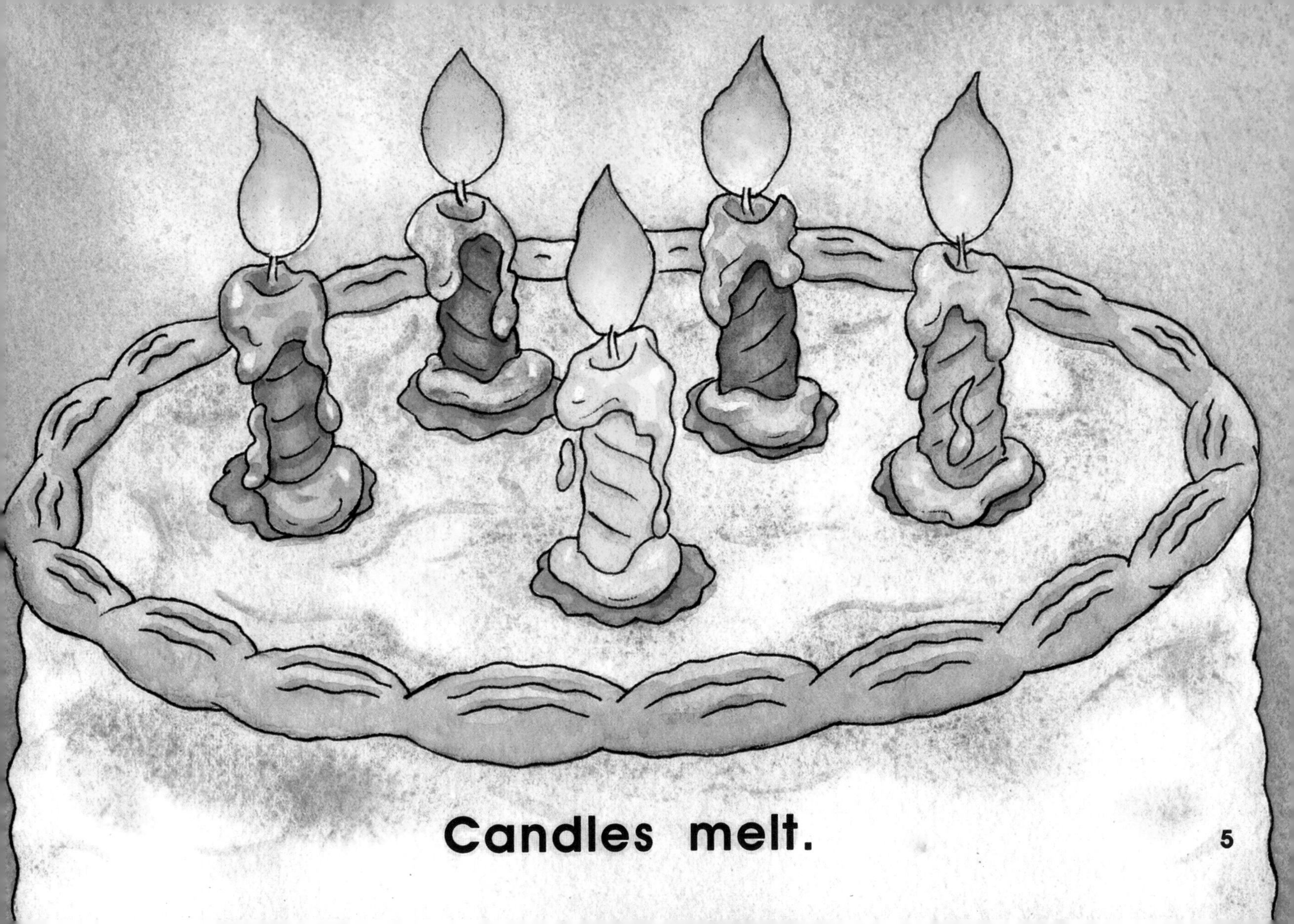

Candles melt.

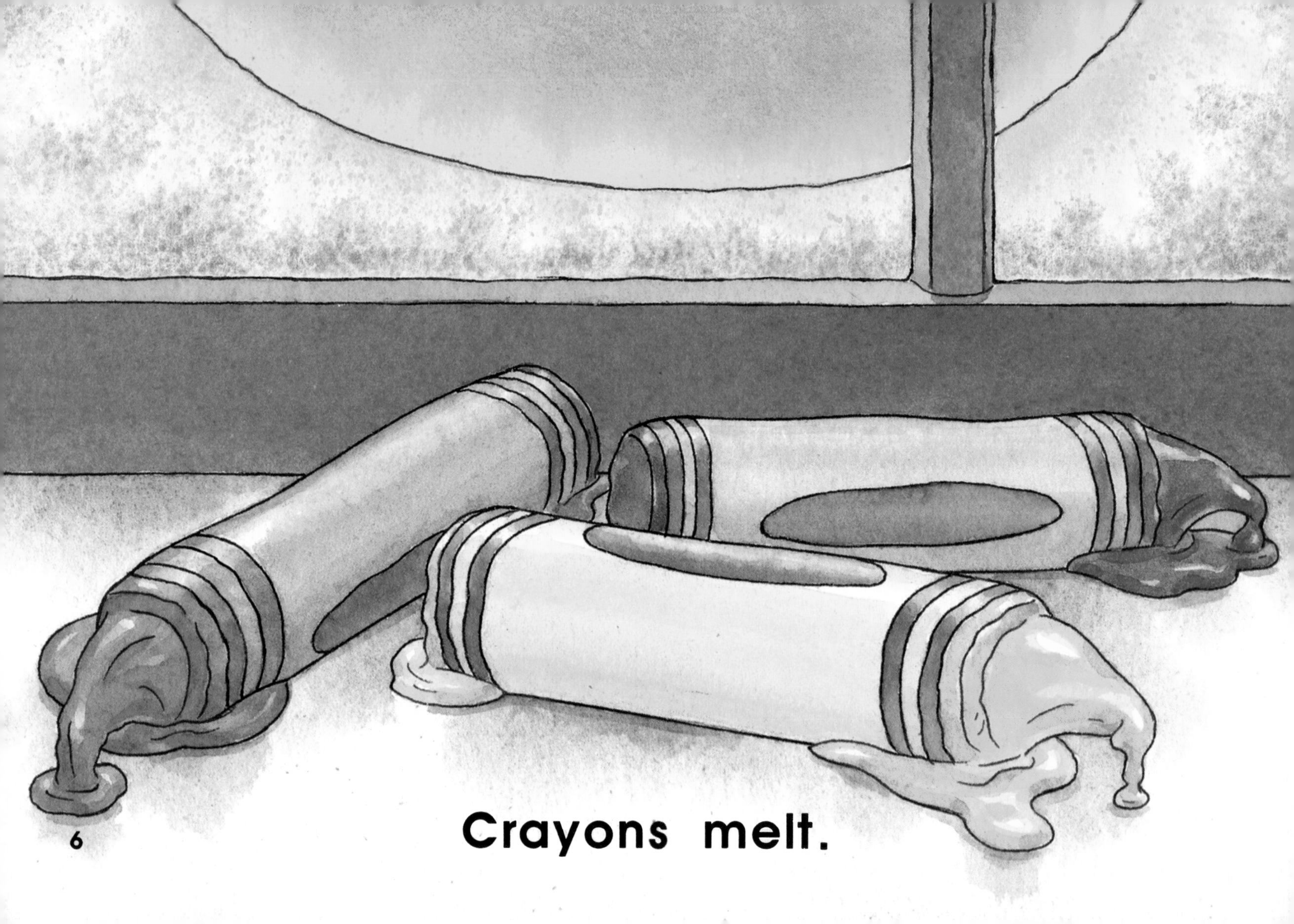

Crayons melt.

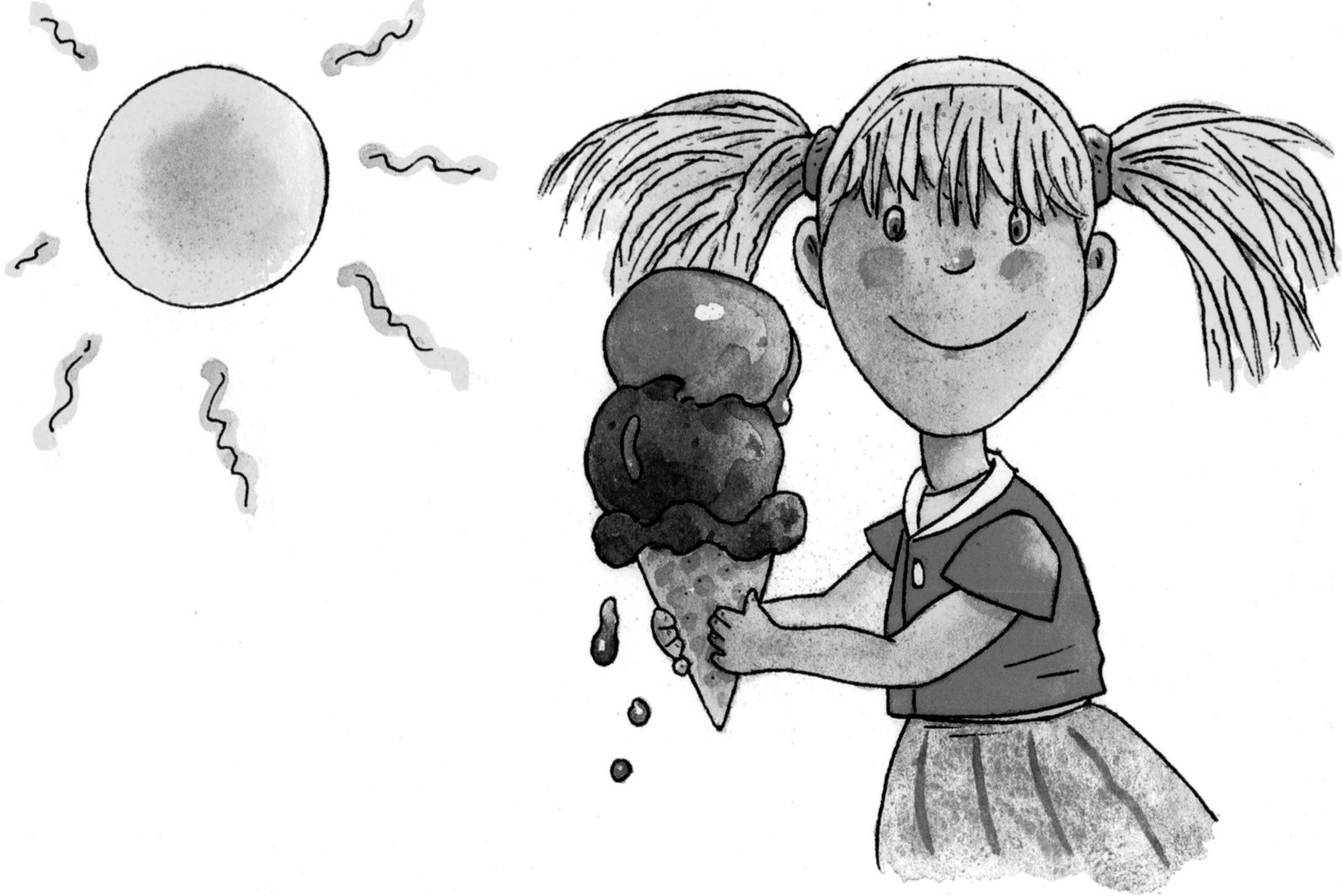

Ice cream melts . . .

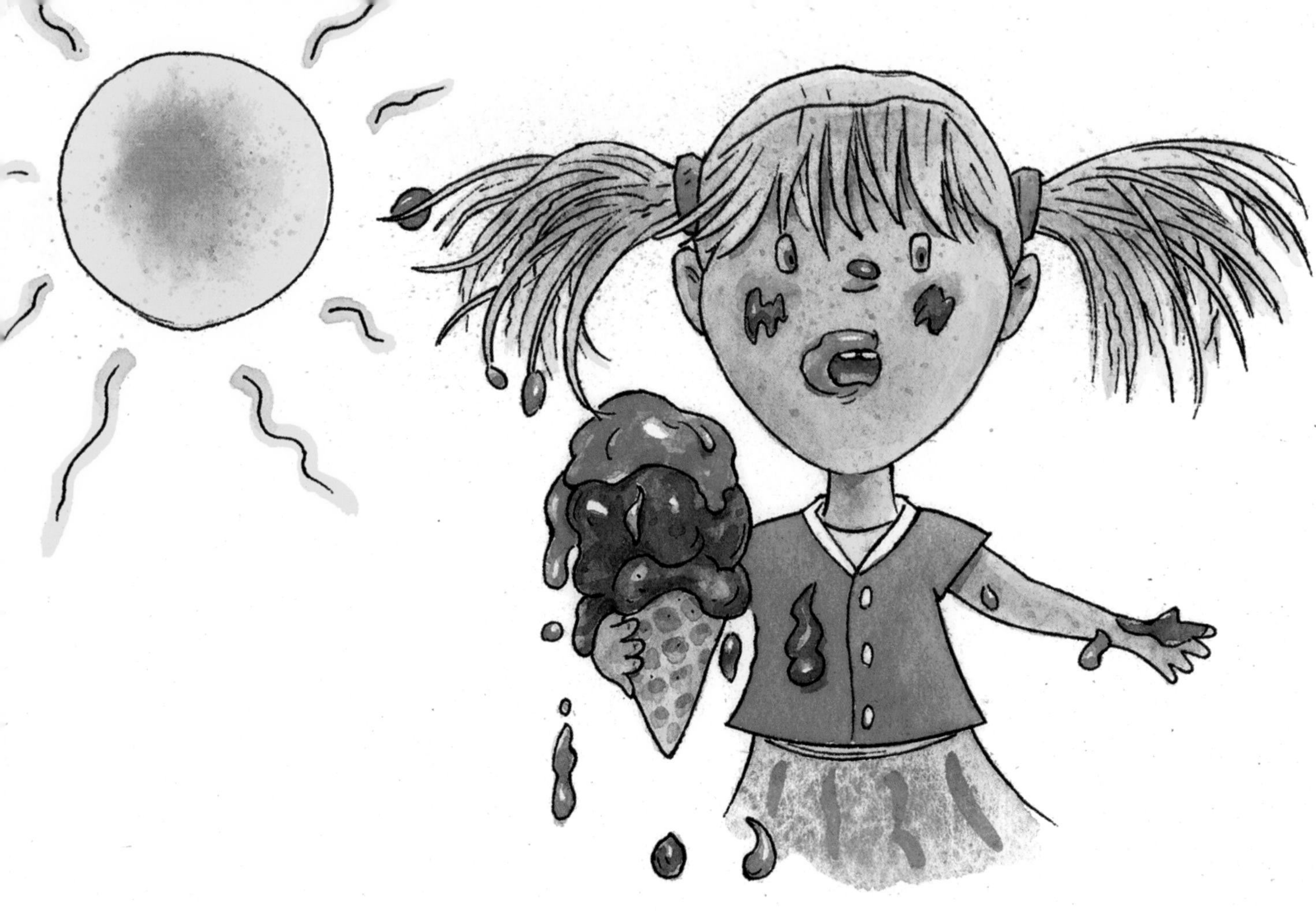

all over me!